From Ann

POCKET IMAGES

# Welshpool

POCKET IMAGES

# Welshpool

Eva B. Bredsdorff

First published 1993
This new pocket edition 2007
Images unchanged from first edition

Nonsuch Publishing Limited
Cirencester Road, Chalford
Stroud, Gloucestershire, GL6 8PE
www.nonsuch-publishing.com

Nonsuch Publishing is an imprint of NPI Media Group



British Library Cataloguing in Publication Data.
A catalogue record for this book is available from the British Library.

ISBN 978-1-84588-434-5

Typesetting and origination by NPI Media Group
Printed in Great Britain

# Contents

# Introduction

Welshpool is a small town of approximately seven thousand inhabitants situated on the Welsh–English border, in the valley of the River Severn, in the county of Montgomeryshire. Today it is a busy market town attracting farmers from near and far for the largest single day market in Wales every Monday. For the visitor the town is the gateway to Wales, with some of the most beautiful countryside of the principality surrounding the town, and several beautiful and interesting places to visit nearby, including the imposing Powis Castle and the Powysland Museum, housed in a renovated warehouse by the canal. There is also the possibility of scenic trips on the Montgomery Canal and the narrow gauge railway to Llanfair Caereinion.

The borough of Welshpool was founded by Gruffudd ap Gwenwynwyn between 1241 and 1245, and was originally known as Burgus de Pola. The town got the name Pool from the several small flooded areas that once existed around the town, but which today have been drained. The name was changed to Welch Pool or Welshpool in the sixteenth century to distinguish it from Poole in Dorset. The spelling varied until the late nineteenth century when Welshpool prevailed. In Welsh the town is called Y Trallwng.

The town was granted a weekly market at its foundation, and by 1292 there were 106 taxpayers. The town was laid out as a typical medieval market town with the main road being High Street, today divided into Broad Street, High Street and Mount Street. Today most buildings date from the eighteenth and nineteenth centuries when the town prospered with different industries including tanning and flannel; as the trading place for the agricultural products of the area and as the communication centre for mid-Wales. Since the Second World War housing estates and industrial areas have sprung up on the outskirts of the town.

The history of Montgomeryshire seems to start in the Mesolithic period (c. 8,500–c. 4,000 BC) from when a few flint implements have been found. The first inhabitants were probably hunters and gatherers. However, as the climate improved the population increased and people took up herding and pastoral agriculture, and during the Neolithic period (c. 4,000–c. 2,000 BC) people turned from a nomadic existence to more settled lives. In the county, settlements, burials and ceremonial sites have been found dating from this period. From the Bronze Age (c. 2,000–c. 700 BC) a large number of items have been found, including bronze axes and spear heads, food vessels and bronze bracelets. Most of the evidence comes from burials, mainly under round barrows, which are often found in the same areas as Neolithic ceremonial sites. In the earlier Bronze Age the dead were buried, but later this changed to cremation with the ashes placed in urns. From the last part of the Bronze Age there are several finds of hoards, mostly bronze axes and spear heads deliberately buried by their owners. There is still not an agreed opinion among archaeologists about the reason for these hoards. From the Iron Age period (c. 700 BC–c. AD 100) the main features are hillforts and smaller enclosed sites. The hillforts are situated on higher ground and on the edges of the Severn Valley, while the smaller enclosed sites are on lower ground and hill slopes. The evidence may indicate the development of a more competitive and violent society. During the same period there is also an increased regionalism in artefact styles and settlement types, which seems to reflect independent and self-sufficient communities.

By AD 75 all the Iron Age communities of Montgomeryshire were absorbed into the Roman empire. To maintain authority the Romans built a network of forts connected by roads. The evidence of the Roman period in Montygomeryshire is therefore dominated by military finds together with a few remnants of rural civilian settlements. Roman artefacts have been found in Welshpool and suggest that the place was a civilian Roman site. From the five hundred years after the Roman withdrawal in AD 400 there are very few finds. It is probable that most native communities continued to exist and function during the following centuries. From Basingwerk in Clwyd to Chepstow in Gwent runs Offa's Dyke, attributed to King Offa of Mercia (AD 757–96). The dyke consists of natural features as well as man-made parts, and the size of it and the effort taken to construct it show its importance. It has been seen as a defensive work but was actually an agreed border between the Mercian king and the Welsh. On the English side it was the economic border of Mercian silver coinage. From aerial photographs it is possible to trace smaller dykes in the area, tending to suggest a number of small independent communities. In the ninth century Scandinavian Vikings reached Wales, and legend has it that a combined army of Anglo-Saxons and the Welsh defeated Danish Vikings in a battle at Buttington near Welshpool in 893.

By 1066 Montgomeryshire was a sparsely populated area. Rural settlements that show field patterns, roads and buildings have been found. The princedom of Powys seems to have been established at about this time, although its exact borders are not known. The earliest evidence of Christianity in the county is an inscribed stone, which has been dated to the late fifth or early sixth century.

The earliest church dates from 1156 while most churches in the county are from the thirteenth century. The Abbey of Strata Marcella was the largest Cistercian monastery in Wales. It was founded in 1170 but was completely demolished during the reign of Henry VIII. During the 200 years following the Battle of Hastings, the area of Montgomeryshire was dominated by local rivalries and struggles with England. The county experienced the consequences of the raids on the English by Llewelyn ap Gruffudd in the thirteenth century, of the conflict between the later Edward III and Queen Isabella and her lover Mortimer, and finally of the last Welsh rebellion by Owain Glyndwr in the fifteenth century. Henry Tudor passed through Montgomeryshire in 1485 on his way to the Battle of Bosworth and is said to have camped outside Welshpool. In 1536, during the reign of Henry VIII, the Acts of Union united Wales and England, and in the process created twelve counties and eleven boroughs, one of which was the county of Montgomeryshire. During the Civil War most people in the area supported Charles I until the county surrendered to Parliamentary forces. Since the political union of Wales and England, Montgomeryshire has been influenced politically and economically by the same developments as the rest of Great Britain, including nonconformity, the Industrial Revolution, poor laws and Chartism, resulting in a modern county that looks to the future while preserving the past.

*Welshpool* does not pretend to tell the history of the town, but rather to give an impression of the bustling life of the inhabitants in a small town in mid-Wales during the last 150 years.

*One*

# Approaching Welshpool

Greetings from Welshpool, 'The Gateway to Wales', welcoming the visitor with pictures of the town and Breidden Hills, the road towards Llanfair Caereinion, Broad Street and Powis Castle.

Breidden Hills and the River Severn. The landscape around Welshpool is dominated by the Severn valley, which is surrounded by the Breiddens and other hills.

Pool Quay, River Severn and the Breiddens. Three miles east of Welshpool, towards Breidden Hills on the left bank of the Severn, was the abbey of Strata Marcella. It belonged to the Cistercian order and was built in 1170. It was later destroyed during the reign of Henry VIII.

Meol-y-Golfa and Breidden Hills. Welshpool lies in the old county of Montgomeryshire and is the headquarters of the district of that name.

Severn Bridge, Welshpool. This bridge crosses the River Severn on the road from Welshpool to Leighton. It was built in 1871 by public subscription and cost £1,780.

Severn Bridge. This photograph dates from before 1961, when floods damaged the bridge.

Kilkewydd Bridge crosses the River Severn at Forden, a small village between Welshpool and Montgomery. The timber bridge was rebuilt with stone in 1862 by the Oswestry and Newtown Railway Company.

The Black Pool is just off the main road from Welshpool to Dolgellau and the Welsh coast. There were several such pools in the area and the town took its original name of Pool from them.

Llanfair Valley, Welshpool. In this photograph from 1956 it is possible to see the tracks of the Welshpool to Llanfair Light Railway.

South-west Welshpool. Today the harvested field has disappeared to make room for residential development.

Welshpool and Breidden Hills. The view is from Powis Castle Park and it is possible to see the Town Hall and St Mary's church.

The Llanfair Road disappears from the right hand side of this photograph on its way towards Llanfair Caereinion.

Welshpool from the south-east, looking towards Powis Castle Park, with the castle in the background and Christ Church on the right.

The town seen from Powis Castle Park, with Christ Church in the foreground and St Mary's church in the background.

*Two*

# The Town

The Cross, in the centre of Welshpool, marks the junction of Broad Street, Severn Street, Church Street and Berriew Street. On a map of the town from 1629 a market cross is indicated. In 1791 the Earl of Powis had a pump erected near the Cross and in 1835 a stone obelisk with three gas lamps was built on the site. This photograph dates from the 1890s.

Broad Street. Another photograph of the Cross, looking down Broad Street. This is the main street of Welshpool, with shops, banks and cafés. On the left hand side can be seen a branch of Stead & Simpson's shoe shop. This photograph dates from the turn of the century.

The Cross and Broad Street. The stone obelisk erected in 1835 still has two of the original three lamps. The top lamp disappeared around 1900 and the two others followed suit later in the twentieth century.

The Cross. This photograph from the 1930s shows the Cross from Broad Street looking towards Severn Street. The street on the right is Berriew Street leading towards Newtown, while to the left is Church Street and the route to Shrewsbury.

Down Broad Street. Broad Street used to be called Pool High Street and was not known as Broad Street until early Victorian days. Today it goes from the Cross to the Town Hall where it runs into High Street.

Broad Street, *c.* 1908. The building on the left is the post office, which, as the sign outside indicates, also housed the public telephone.

Broad Street, between 1910 and 1913. On the front of the fourth house on the left hand side of the photograph is a large royal coat of arms. This belonged to the tailoring and outfitting business of the Wall family. In 1832 Mr David Wall met the Duchess of Kent and Princess Victoria when they visited Powis Castle. After this meeting his business supplied the royal household with Welsh flannel and was allowed to display the royal arms.

The corner of Broad Street and Berriew Street. The black and white corner house was demolished in 1876. The site was occupied by the North and South Wales Bank until 1908, when it became the Midland Bank.and later HSBC

Broad Street and High Street, from further up Broad Street towards the Town Hall and the beginning of High Street. Some of the many cafés and public houses of the town can be seen: the Welshpool Coffee House, the Temperance Hotel and the Victoria Vaults. This photograph dates from between 1910 and 1913.

Broad Street in the 1950s. Several of the shops shown here are still in business today. The first shop on the right hand side is W.H. Smith, which has moved farther down the street since then. Boots the Chemist is still in the same place, although it has now also acquired the neighbouring building.

Raven Street. This photograph, from the beginning of the twentieth century, is taken from Raven Square, looking towards the town. The house in the middle of the picture was The Black Lion Inn.

*Opposite below:* Lledan Crescent, Brook Street, 1931. This row of houses was built in the 1820s and was named after the Lledan brook running close by. As the ground floor of the houses was below street level and the brook overflowed at times, floods like the one in the photograph happened quite often. The buildings were demolished in 1972 and the site has been occupied by Welshpool Library since 1983.

Severn Street, looking towards the Cross. The spelling of the town as Welch Pool or Welshpool alternated in documents until modern times, when the spelling of Welshpool was standardized.

Severn Street at the turn of the twentieth century. The street was originally known as Caus Street, and most houses were private residences built for prosperous men. Out of the twenty-two private telephones in the town in 1922, ten belonged to houses in Severn Street.

Church Street at the Cross, *c.* 1880. On the right hand side is the sign for The Coach and Horses pub, which later became Morris, Marshall and Poole Auctioneers.

Church Street, looking towards St Mary's church. In the centre is a sign for Clive cinema, which was housed in an old flannel factory from 1924.

Church Street. On the right hand side is the entrance to The Bull inn, which later became the Queen's Hotel. There seems to have been an inn or hotel on this site since the sixteenth century.

Church Bank. The three buildings are St Mary's church, Grace Evans's Cottage (sometimes known as Lady Nithdale's Cottage) and the Museum Cottage. This photograph was taken before the Powysland Museum was built here in 1874.

*Left*: Church Street continues into Salop Road. The road on the left is Gungrog Road, which leads to the Victoria Memorial Hospital.

*Below*: Berriew Street, once called Llangollen or Llangolwyn Street, looking towards the Cross. This photograph was taken at the turn of the century and shows the busy street with many shops and public houses.

*Three*

# Buildings

Christ Church, from Powis Castle Park. The foundation stone was laid on 5 November 1839 to celebrate the coming of age of Edward James, Viscount Clive, later 3rd Earl of Powis.

Christ Church from the south-west. This is still the family church of the Earls of Powis.

*Right*: The interior of Christ Church, looking towards the altar.

*Below*: St Mary's parish church from Church Street. The church was founded by Cynfelyn and was probably dedicated to him, but was later rededicated to St Mary of the Salutation. Parts of the building date from the thirteenth century, but many alterations were made in the following centuries. The church was partly rebuilt in the eighteenth century.

St Mary's church from Union Street. One of the smaller houses on the left was the old almshouse, said to have been founded by Thomas Parry in 1741. It had eight rooms and was closed down in the first or second decade of the twentieth century.

St Mary's church with Lledan brook in the foreground. This was one of the two brooks in the town, the other being Llyndu stream. They were both used as sewers and posed a threat to the health of the population. This was proved in 1848 when Welshpool was hit by the worst cholera epidemic in North Wales.

St Mary's church from Church Bank. On the right is the entrance to the old Powysland Museum and the Museum Cottage.

The interior of St Mary's church, looking towards the altar and the stained glass east window, one of the most magnificent in the area.

Grace Evans's Cottage. Lord Nithsdale supported James II and was therefore arrested, accused of treason and imprisoned in the Tower of London. His wife, who was a daughter of the first Marquis of Powis, decided to help her husband. With her maid-in-waiting, Grace Evans, she managed to free the lord in 1716 and they all fled to France. Whether Grace returned to Welshpool and died here or ended her days in France is not known.

Grace Evans's Cottage is said to have been given to Grace by Lord Nithsdale in gratitude for his rescue. It has also been known as the Verger's House, as it was the home of church officials of St Mary's church for many years.

The Museum Cottage on Church Bank. Although the caption reads 'Powys-land Museum', the picture was actually taken before the museum was built. The cottage became the home of the museum caretaker.

The Powysland Museum was built in 1874 by the Powysland Club, a local history society founded in 1867. It was a purpose-built museum and was enlarged during the following decades. The collection consisted of geology, archaeology and social history items from all over the world. In 1990 most of the Powysland collection was moved to a restored and renovated warehouse by the Montgomery Canal.

The Old Crib, demolished in 1899, stood behind Park Lane House. During the reign of Charles II it was used as a prison for several Quakers. They lived in terrible conditions with little food and poor hygiene.

The Old or Upper Packhorse Inn stood in Mount Street until it was demolished shortly after the phone box was installed. It may have dated from the sixteenth century and was the meeting point of traders when the Pool fairs were held at Raven Square.

Sergeants' Row on Severn Street was built to accommodate the families of militia sergeants during the Napoleonic Wars of the nineteenth century. They were built by the Earl of Powis, who was also in charge of the militia. Later the houses were given to veterans of the Napoleonic Wars.

*Right:* Mansion House, 24 Severn Street, was built by Richard Griffiths at the beginning of the nineteenth century. It is one of the most imposing buildings in Severn Street.

*Below:* Park Lane House, 7 High Street, is another typical Regency building.

*Above*: Nos 10–11 High Street, said to date from the sixteenth century. There is a block of wood inside the building which has 'D.P. Old Oliver' studded in nails on it. This has been interpreted as God Strafe Old Oliver, an understandable sentiment for a town of royalist loyalties.

Left: No. 34 High Street is another imposing house dating from the Regency period.

The old Town Hall. On the Bleaze map of 1629 there are two buildings standing in the middle of what is now Broad Street. The one by the Cross was the Market Hall, which had a room above used for Great Sessions and other courts. In 1758 the floor of this room collapsed and six people were killed. As a consequence the Market Hall was pulled down. The courts and the market were moved to the other building in the street, called either the Town Hall or the Guildhall. In 1795 the floor collapsed here as well. In the following year funds were raised to rebuild the Town Hall, and the work was finished in 1804.

*Above:* The new Town Hall. Although the old Town Hall was further enlarged in 1836 it was soon considered too small and was demolished. The new Town Hall was built in 1873 for £6,000.

*Left:* The Smithfield Fountain in the Smithfield Market was removed before the Second World War.

*Four*

# Trade

Broad Street is the main shopping street of Welshpool, seen here in the early twentieth century. On the right is the Star Tea Co. Ltd. The large building farther down was known as Trade Hall.

THE CHOICEST

# NEW SEASON'S TEAS GROWN

Are now being offered by

## The STAR TEA COMPANY,

LIMITED,

TEA EXPERTS & BLENDERS.

| GOOD FAMILY TEA | CHOICEST BLEND PEKOE SOUCHONG. | CEYLON AND INDIAN PEKOE |
| --- | --- | --- |
| Per 1/- lb. | Per 1/4 lb. | Per 1/6 lb. |

| SUPERB INDIAN & CEYLON BLEND | RICH CEYLON AND INDIAN ORANGE PEKOE |
| --- | --- |
| Per 1/8 lb. | Per 1/10 lb. |

For Delicious Aroma, Purity and Refinement, our Teas are Unexcelled.

ONLY ADDRESS IN THE TOWN:—

## THE STAR TEA CO., Ltd.,

Tea Merchants, General Grocers and
Purveyors of High-Class Provisions,

19, Broad Street, WELSHPOOL.

[Please Turn Over.

Advert for the Star Tea Co. Ltd. The Star chain store was the first of its kind in Welshpool, opening before the First World War.

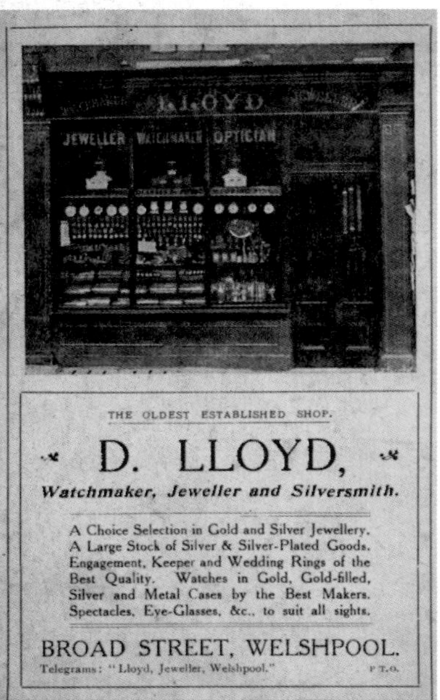


THE OLDEST ESTABLISHED SHOP.

D. LLOYD,

**Watchmaker, Jeweller and Silversmith.**

A Choice Selection in Gold and Silver Jewellery. A Large Stock of Silver & Silver-Plated Goods. Engagement, Keeper and Wedding Rings of the Best Quality. Watches in Gold, Gold-filled, Silver and Metal Cases by the Best Makers. Spectacles, Eye-Glasses, &c., to suit all sights.

BROAD STREET, WELSHPOOL.

Telegrams: "Lloyd, Jeweller, Welshpool." P.T.O.

*Above*: Broad Street on a market day, *c.* 1950. On the left are two shoe shops, Mortons and Stead & Simpsons. Boots the Chemist is on the right hand side of the street.

*Left*: Advertising card for D. Lloyd, watchmaker and jeweller.

*Above*: Nos 7–8 Broad Street: D. Lloyd's shop and A.E. Bond the confectioner.

*Right*: No. 7 Broad Street: D. Lloyd, watchmaker, jeweller and silversmith.

No. 9 Broad Street. These premises were a grocers shop until D. Lloyd moved his business here from 7 Broad Street in the 1890s.

*Above*: No. 40 Broad Street, Miss Holmes's wool shop. To the left is Harding's fish shop.

*Right*: Nos 21–2 Broad Street, Watson's grocers shop. The house was built in 1736 and has a long history of being a grocers shop. Next to it is W.H. Smith, which today has moved further up the street.

*Above*: Nos 5–6 High Street. This house was built in the eighteenth century and was formerly called the Red House. Since the mid-eighteenth century it has been occupied by cabinet makers. In 1910 J.H. Anderson & Son had their cabinet makers and photographers business here. Today it is Anderson's Antiques.

*Left*: Nos 9–10 High Street. These two shops belonged to W.N. Owen, cabinet maker, and E. Richards, hairdresser.

Nos 9–10 High Street. In the eighteenth century this was The Upper Sun public house, next to The Cross Keys inn. In the 1920s it was renovated and opened as a café, Prentice Traders.

Nos 20–2 High Street. Plas Goch Houses were built in the eighteenth century and, like many other houses in the town, were at one time owned by Powis Castle.

*Left*: No. 47 High Street. Before 1886 this building was owned by the Welshpool Coffee House Ltd, serving non-alcoholic beverages in the Cocoa Rooms. In 1886 Edward Wyke bought the building and it became a grocers shop.

*Below*: Advert card for T.A. Clemson. In the 1940s the grocers shop at 47 High Street was run by Mr T.A. Clemson. It later became Phillips's Store.

T. A. CLEMSON,

FAMILY GROCER,

WELSHPOOL.

WHITBREAD'S BEER & STOUT IN BOTTLES.

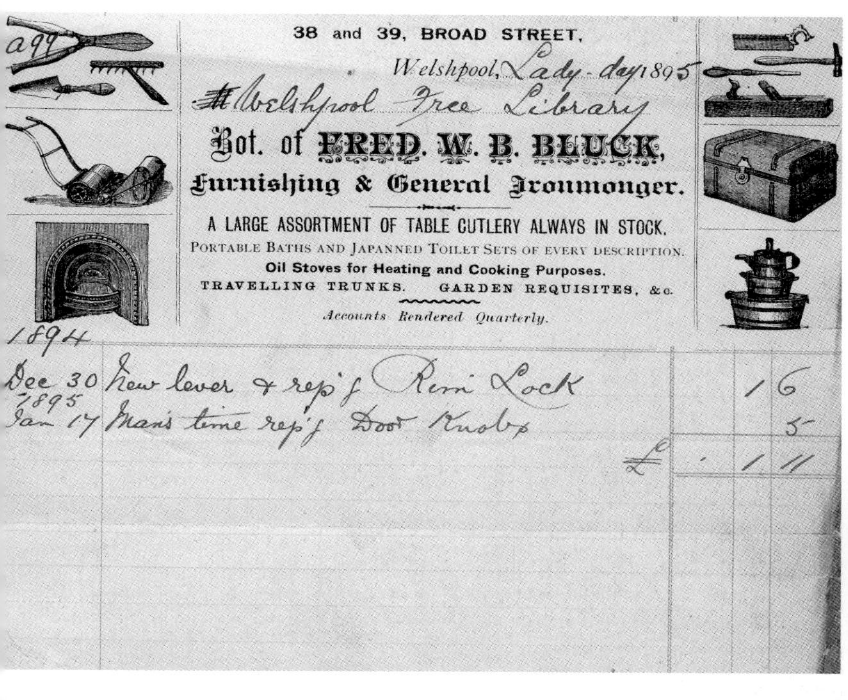

38 and 39, BROAD STREET,

Welshpool, Lady-day 1895

The Welshpool Free Library

Bot. of FRED. W. B. BLUCK,

Furnishing & General Ironmonger.

A LARGE ASSORTMENT OF TABLE CUTLERY ALWAYS IN STOCK.

PORTABLE BATHS AND JAPANNED TOILET SETS OF EVERY DESCRIPTION.

Oil Stoves for Heating and Cooking Purposes.

TRAVELLING TRUNKS. GARDEN REQUISITES, &c.

*Accounts Rendered Quarterly.*

| | | | |
|---|---|---|---|
| 1894 Dec 30 | New lever & rep'g Rim Lock | 1 | 6 |
| 1895 Jan 17 | Man's time rep'g Door Knobs | | 5 |
| | £ . | 1 | 11 |

*Above:* A bill, dated 1895, from Fred W.B. Bluck, furnishing and general ironmonger of 38–9 Broad Street. It shows the large variety of goods available. Notice especially the Japanned toilet sets.

*Right:* A bill from William Gwilt. Mr Gwilt was a very versatile man–a plumber, glazier and painter, and, according to the bill, he worked for the Welsh Calvinistic Methodist chapel in 1877.

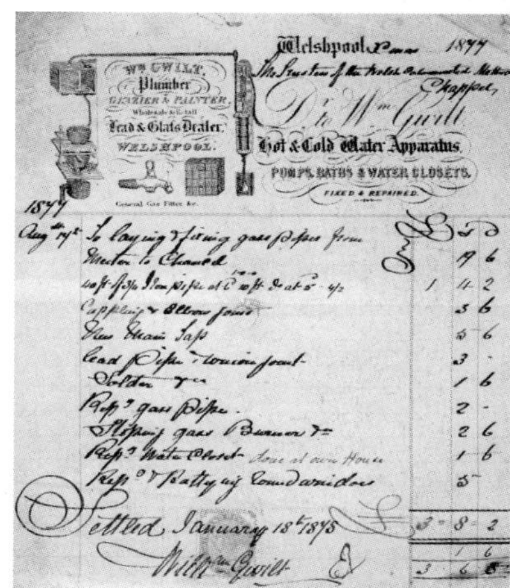

Welshpool [illegible] 1877

The Trustees of the Welsh [illegible] Methodist Chappel,

Dr. to Wm Gwilt

Wm GWILT, Plumber, Glazier & Painter, Wholesale & Retail Lead & Glass Dealer, Welshpool.

Hot & Cold Water Apparatus, Pumps, Baths & Water Closets, Fixed & Repaired.

General Gas Fitter &c.

| 1877 | | £ | s | d |
|---|---|---|---|---|
| Aug 14th | To laying & fixing gass pipes from Meter to Chapel | | 19 | 6 |
| | [illegible] | 1 | 4 | 2 |
| | Coppling & Elbow joint | | 3 | 6 |
| | New Main Tap | | 5 | 6 |
| | Lead pipe & union joint | | 3 | - |
| | Solder &c | | 1 | 6 |
| | Repg gass pipe | | 2 | - |
| | Stopping gass Burner &c | | 2 | 6 |
| | Repg Water Closet done at own House | | 1 | 6 |
| | Repg & [illegible] | | 5 | |
| | | 3 | 8 | 2 |
| | | | 1 | 6 |
| | | 3 | 6 | 8 |

Settled January 18th 1878

Willm Gwilt

Later
G.E. Reese

*Left*: No. 7 Church Street, the tobacconist shop of Mrs Sayce. It was known as the 'Black Boy shop', referring to the figure of a smoking Indian standing over the door.

*Below*: The Wool Warehouse on Church Bank and the Seed Warehouse on Church Street, both owned by Watkin & Jones, wool, seed and manure merchants. The warehouse on Church Bank was originally a flannel factory and was demolished around 1960. The other warehouse still exists.

WOOL WAREHOUSE, CHURCH BANK.

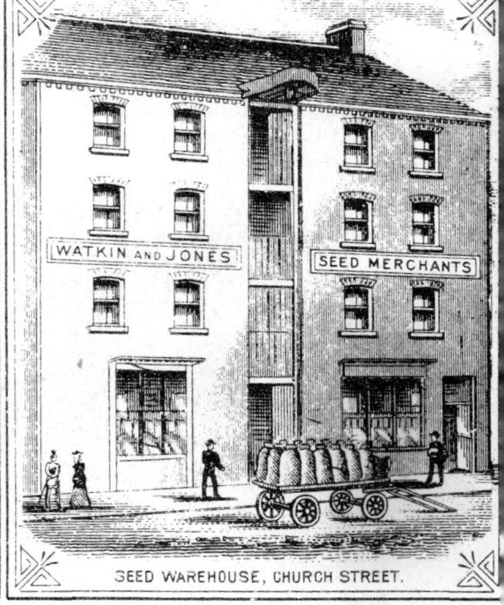


SEED WAREHOUSE, CHURCH STREET.

The annexe to 2 Church Bank was the workshop of Charlie Parry, who was the last white cooper to trade in Welshpool. A white cooper made items specifically for dairying.

Glandwr on Rt before Hendre was built ↓

Salop Road, *c.* 1910. This photograph shows two of the businesses in the street: C.W. Jones, general store, on the left and on the right the Powis Arms pub.

*Left*: No. 25 Severn Street, a building that dates from the early nineteenth century. It was the offices of Norman R. Lloyd and Co., auctioneers and valuers.

*Below*: The old *County Times* offices in Severn Street. In 1893 the County Times, a local newspaper, was founded by David Rowlands and Samuel Salter. Its first offices were in Berriew Street, but in 1915 it moved to Severn Street. In the 1960s the newspaper moved again, to High Street, and in 1963 a post office was opened on this site.

G. E. Reese was a Traveller for the 'County Times'

No. 17 Berriew Street, and T.J. Evans's shop in 1910. This was an ironmongers shop that sold a wide variety of goods.

The Old or Upper Packhorse inn, a sixteenth-century building on Mount Street. This was a popular meeting place for traders and farmers on market days.

BULL · HOTEL

Hotel Omnibus meets all trains and posting in all its branches.

Grand coffee, commercial, smoking & billiard rooms. Suites of apartments.

Horses & Carriages of every description supplied.

Ordinary daily 1 P.M.

MISS JENKINS, MANAGERESS. No

Telegraphic Address: "Bull, Welshpool."

1899 Sept

Brought Forward
Breakfasts
Luncheons
Dinners
Teas
Suppers
Wines
Spirits
Beer
Mineral Waters
Cigars
Apartments
Attendance
Fires
Lights
Baths
Stationery, &c.
Paid out
Visitors' Washing
Servants' Board
Sundries
Carried Forward

1 Bott Best Port 4-6

Pd … Edwards Sept 7/99

*Above*: The Grapes Inn at Waterloo Place in Salop Road. This is a pub with a homely atmosphere.

*Left*: The Bull Hotel stood in Church Street, and there is evidence that it has existed since at least the sixteenth century.

*Opposite below*: Advertising postcard for the Queen's Hotel. The hotel was pulled down at the beginning of the 1960s and today there is a National Milk Bar on the site.

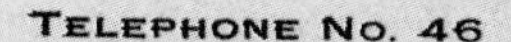

TELEPHONE No. 46 TELEGRAMS: "QUEENS"

FREE HOUSE
FULLY LICENSED

THE QUEEN'S HOTEL

PROP.: WM. GEORGE WEBSTER

Family and Commercial

CHURCH STREET, WELSHPOOL

Advertising card for the Queen's Hotel. On the back it says, 'The well-known Tourist Resort on the main road from the West Midlands to the Cambrian Coast. Formerly "The Bull", a celebrated hostelry dating from the Fifteenth Century.'

The Queen's Hotel, Church Street. In 1654 there were ninety-eight public houses in Welshpool. By the nineteenth century the number had fallen to between thirty and forty, while today Welshpool has thirteen.

Edw^d. Bayley
OAK INN, Pool

Neat Poſt Chaiſes

| | L | S | D |
|---|---|---|---|
| Eating | | | |
| Coffee & Tea | | | |
| Wine | | | |
| Brandy & Rum | | | |
| Punch | | | |
| Cyder & Perry | | | |
| Malt Liquor &c | | | |
| Servants Eating | | | |
| Ditto's Liquor | | | |
| Smith | | | |
| Washing | | | |
| Hay & Corn | | | |

*Right*: A bill from The Oak Inn, Pool. This is another old public house, today called The Royal Oak. It is said to have acquired its name from a large oak tree that stood in the middle of the street.

*Below*: The Royal Oak Hotel. The word 'royal' is said to have been added because local Jacobite supporters held meetings in the building.

The Seven Stars Inn. This public house gave its name to the Welshpool to Llanfair Light Railway station (see p. 88), but was pulled down in 1902 to make way for the railway.

*Five*

# Transport

Leighton Gate. Turnpikes or toll-gates were erected to charge users of the road so as to help the local parishes finance the upkeep and improvement of the roads. In 1769 the first Turnpike Act in Montgomeryshire was passed through Parliament. For administrative purposes the county was divided into three districts. The first covered the roads of the area of Welshpool, Newtown and Llanidloes; the second those of Welshpool and Machynlleth; and the third the Llanfyllin/ Llansantffraid to Welshpool and Oswestry road.

Ceunant Gate. In the 1769 Act the toll charges were, 'Coaches and vehicles of that class–3d. per beast drawing; Carts and wains–2d. per beast drawing; Horses and asses laden or unladen–1d. when not drawing; Cattle–10d. per score; Smaller animals: calves, sheep and pigs–5d. per score.' These charges were later raised.

Llanfair Road Gate. In 1834 the administration was made easier by an Act that grouped roads together according to the area they served. The tolls were changed as well: 'Vehicle of coach class–1s. per beast drawing; Waggon–8d. per beast drawing; Horse and mule–2d. when not drawing; Ass–1d. when not drawing; For every carriage moved or propelled or set or kept in motion by steam or machinery or any other power or agency than animal power–2s. 6d. per wheel for each wheel thereof.' Almost all of the county's roads were freed from tolls by 1886.

*Opposite above*: Pool Quay. The River Severn was navigable to this point and the 120 miles from Bristol were used by boats until the 1820s. From Bristol were imported wine, tobacco, oil, shot, brassware and soap; and from places along the river came ironware, textiles, earthenware, cider, salt and coal. During the 1820s the navigation of the river was threatened by low water, but the building of the Montgomery Canal allowed Pool Quay to uphold its status as a trading centre, although it was less important than before.

*Opposite below*: Belan Locks, near Welshpool, on the Montgomery Canal, *c*. 1930.

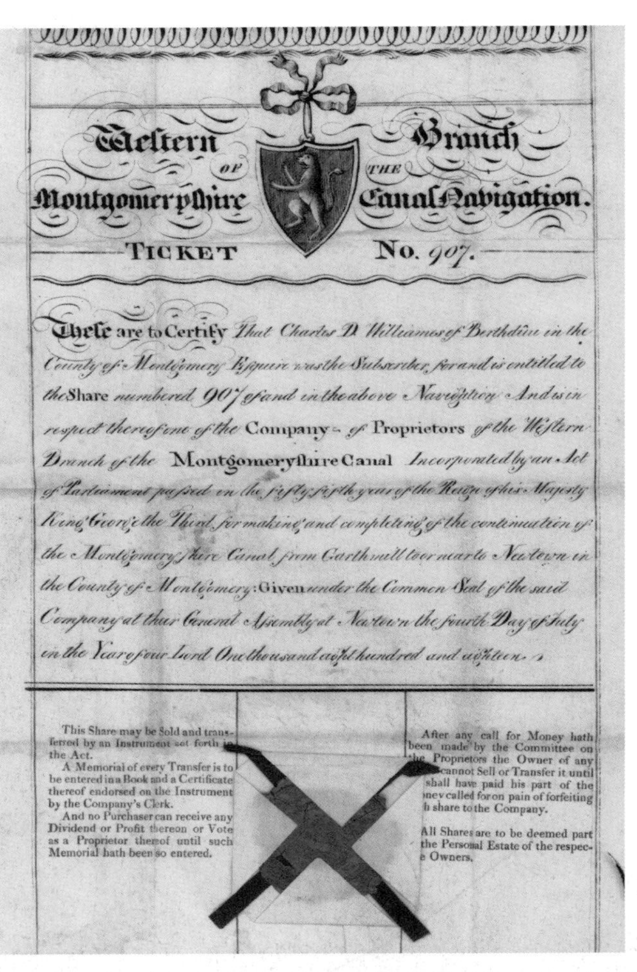

Western Branch of the Montgomeryshire Canal Navigation.

TICKET No. 907.

These are to Certify That Charles D. Williames of Berthddu in the County of Montgomery Esquire was the Subscriber for and is entitled to the Share numbered 907 of and in the above Navigation And is in respect thereof one of the Company of Proprietors of the Western Branch of the Montgomeryshire Canal Incorporated by an Act of Parliament passed in the fifty fifth year of the Reign of his Majesty King George the Third for making and completing of the continuation of the Montgomeryshire Canal from Garthmill to or near to Newtown in the County of Montgomery: Given under the Common Seal of the said Company at their General Assembly at Newtown the fourth Day of July in the Year of our Lord One thousand eight hundred and eighteen.

This Share may be Sold and transferred by an Instrument set forth in the Act.

A Memorial of every Transfer is to be entered in a Book and a Certificate thereof endorsed on the Instrument by the Company's Clerk.

And no Purchaser can receive any Dividend or Profit thereon or Vote as a Proprietor thereof until such Memorial hath been so entered.

After any call for Money hath been made by the Committee on the Proprietors the Owner of any ... cannot Sell or Transfer it until ... shall have paid his part of the ...ney called for on pain of forfeiting ...h share to the Company.

All Shares are to be deemed part ... the Personal Estate of the respec...e Owners.

Share No. 907–the western branch of the Montgomery Canal. The Montgomeryshire Canal Act of March 1794 allowed for the building of a canal from or near Porthywaen Lime Rocks through Welshpool, Berriew, Garthmyl and Newtown, with two arms from Porthywaen to Llanymynech Lime Rocks and from Burgedin to the Sarnau Crowner Bridge. Between 1794 and 1797 when the budget of £71,000 was exhausted, 18½ miles were completed, including the waterway between Welshpool and Garthmyl and the arm to Guilsfield. Not until 1815, however, was work continued, when the Western Branch Act allowed the raising of more funds for work on the original canal, now called the eastern branch. A further act in 1821 enabled improvements to the eastern branch. By 1821 the western branch had been completed.

Canal Company seal from a share certificate of the original Montgomery Canal Company, 1794.

Shropshire Union Railways and Canal Company sign, dated 1901. An act passed in August 1846 allowed the canal to be sold to the Shropshire Union Railways and Canal Company, with the idea of constructing a railway along the course of the canal in the future. In 1847 the canal was leased to the London & North Western Railway company and although the idea of building a railway was mooted it was finally dropped in 1861, when the Cambrian Railways' Oswestry to Newtown line was opened.

The Montgomery Canal along Berriew Road, looking towards Welshpool, 1960. In 1944 an Abandonment Act prohibited the navigation of the canal, but in 1987 an Enabling Act repealed this and allowed the British Waterways Board to start restoration work. Today it is a beautiful nature reserve, a centre for recreation and an important part of the industrial heritage of the area.

The Welshpool lock.

*Right*: An old view of the canal. The Montgomery Canal has been called an agricultural rather than an industrial waterway. Its aim was not to make a profit as a means of transport, but to secure cheap and dependable transportation of heavy goods for the landowners along or near the canal. It was an alternative to road transport, which was very expensive because of the tolls.

*Below*: The canal today. The waterway helped to turn the upper Severn valley into agricultural land, made raw materials economically accessible and opened up new markets.

A view from Severn Bridge towards the south-west of Welshpool, at the beginning of the twentieth century. The main trade of the canal was limestone, which produced a very efficient fertilizer when burnt with coal. Limestone and coal were transported down the canal and deposited at the numerous lime kilns built along the canal. Coal was also transported for industrial and household uses. There were seventeen specialized coal wharves, one of them being Hollybush wharf which can be seen in this photograph. One of the most important exports from the area was timber, which had been transported down the River Severn since at least the thirteenth century. The timber trade was very important for the landowners in Montgomeryshire and the canal was a reliable means of transportation. To the right can be seen the large wheel of the corn mill still in place.

Building the Severn Street bridge in 1900. Until this time there seems to have been a much steeper bridge across the canal, which was a terrible strain on the horses pulling the loaded lorries between the town and the station. However, in 1900 a local man, Charles Edward Howell, instigated and paid for the rebuilding of the bridge in red bricks with sandstone copings, thus making the gradients easier.

The Welshpool Yard or Canal Company warehouse. Many goods were transported up and down the canal, including grain, dairy products and luxury wares, and between 1840 and 1850 there seem to have been about thirty warehouses along the canal storing goods for import as well as export. The earliest part of the Welshpool Yard warehouse was built at the beginning of the nineteenth century and the rest was added in the 1880s. The building has always been a warehouse, in the beginning associated with the canal but later owned by different local firms—during the 1930s and 1940s by Morgan Edwards Ltd.

The canal wharf in 1946.

Morris's Foundry Yard. The canal also generated different industries. During the first fifty years of its existence there were on its banks two flannel factories, one foundry, five malting and brewing houses, one gasworks, two corn mills and four joiners' workshops, all using the water of the canal or the canal feeders.

*Above*: The Welshpool Company for the manufacture of flannel by steam. This factory was built in 1834 and closed down later, but was reopened in 1883 by Sir Pryce Pryce Jones of Newtown under the name of Powysland Tweed and Flannel Mills. It closed in 1900, then became a tannery, and from 1914 to 1915 it was an ordnance factory employing 400–500 people. Later it was a motorcycle factory. The building was finally demolished in 1930.

*Left*: During very hard winters the canal has been known to freeze, and local children have been able to play on the ice.

Welshpool railway station in 1880. During the middle of the nineteenth century, after the successful opening of the Manchester to Liverpool railway line in 1830, a railway mania swept over Great Britain. It reached its climax on Sunday 30 November 1845, when 1,263 schemes representing £560,000,000 were presented to Parliament. Only 272 of these were approved by Parliament. Among them was one proposing the conversion of the Montgomery Canal to a railway line. However, during the 1850s and 1860s, out of all these schemes emerged the lines that together made up the Cambrian Railways Company. This was the largest of the independent Welsh railways, covering three hundred miles of track and going through some of the most beautiful countryside in the British Isles. In 1859 the line from Llanidloes to Newtown was opened, and in 1860 this was followed by the line from Oswestry to Newtown via Welshpool.

*Left*: Mrs Anne Warburton Owen, an important landowner in the area and a keen supporter of the railway. The ceremony of the cutting of the first sod on the Llanidloes to Newtown line should have been performed by Mrs Owen of Glansevern, but as she read about her participation in the Shrewsbury Chronicle before she had been asked she refused to take part, and the ceremony was performed by Mr G.H. Whalley. However, four years later Mrs Owen agreed to open the line. She also opened the Oswestry to Newtown line.

*Below*: Welshpool railway station, built in 1860 and seen here in 1978. It is no longer used as a station.

Winners of the Cambrian Railway Shield, *c.* 1915. The shield was awarded for proficiency in first aid. In 1864 the Cambrian Railways Company obtained powers to combine and run the Llanidloes to Newtown, Oswestry to Newtown, Newtown to Machynlleth and Oswestry, Ellesmere and Whitchurch lines. In 1904 the company was given royal assent to amalgamate with the Mid-Wales Railway Company.

Winners of the Cambrian Railway Shield, 1915. During the First World War all railways were brought under state control. In 1922 all independent railways in Wales, including the Cambrian Railways Company, were taken over by the Great Western Railway Company. In 1948 the railways were nationalized, and this company became part of British Rail.

No. 164

**WELSHPOOL AND LLANFAIR LIGHT RAILWAY COMPANY.**

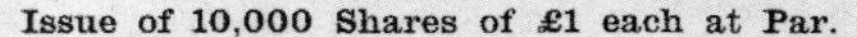

**Issue of 10,000 Shares of £1 each at Par.**

Payable 2/6 per Share on application, 2/6 per Share on allotment, and by further calls of not exceeding 5/- per Share at intervals of not less than three months with the option of payment in full on allotment.

**ALLOTMENT LETTER.**

To Mr Robert Owen and Miss Mary Newell Owen. Welshpool

Sir ~~or~~ and Madam,

I am directed to inform you that in accordance with your application the Directors have allotted you 20 Shares of £1 each in this Company.

You paid £ 2-10-0 on application, and I beg to inform you that a like sum being the 2/6 per Share payable on allotment will become due from you at the expiration of one month from the date of this letter, and must then be paid to the North and South Wales Bank, Limited, at Welshpool or Llanfair; or to Lloyds Bank, Limited, Welshpool

Upon payment of the instalments and upon presentation of this document at the Office of the Company, you will be entitled to receive a Certificate under the Company's Seal.

I am,
Your obedient Servant,
John Evans
Secretary.

24, Broad Street,
Welshpool,
8th February, 1900.

No. 164

**Welshpool and Llanfair Light Railway Company.**

**BANKERS' RECEIPT.**

Received the 13th day of March 1900, on account of The Welshpool and Llanfair Light Railway Company, the sum of £ ~~2-10-0~~ £10:– ~~being the sum of 2s. 6d. per Share, payable on allotment~~ of 20 Shares.
(Ten pounds)

For LLOYDS BANK, LIMITED.
~~For NORTH AND SOUTH WALES BANK, LIMITED.~~

A/c £10:–
£ ~~2~~ : ~~10~~ : 0

H. W. Evetts
Cashier

The following order to be detached and retained by the Bankers.

Form must be presented entire to the Bankers on payment of the instalment.

Allotment letter of the Welshpool and Llanfair Light Railway Company. In 1862 the first proposal of a railway between Welshpool and Llanfair Caereinion was suggested, but owing to politics, local differences and financial problems the plans were changed, dropped and revived for the next thirty-five years. However, the passing of the Light Railway Act by Parliament in August 1896 relaxed the laws for the building and running of light railway lines and this inspired new plans to be made. On 10 March 1898 a meeting of interested parties from the area nominated the first directors of the Welshpool and Llanfair Caereinion Light Railway Company. For the next two years negotiations took place with the Cambrian Railways company for the building and running of the line, and a ninety-nine year agreement was reached.

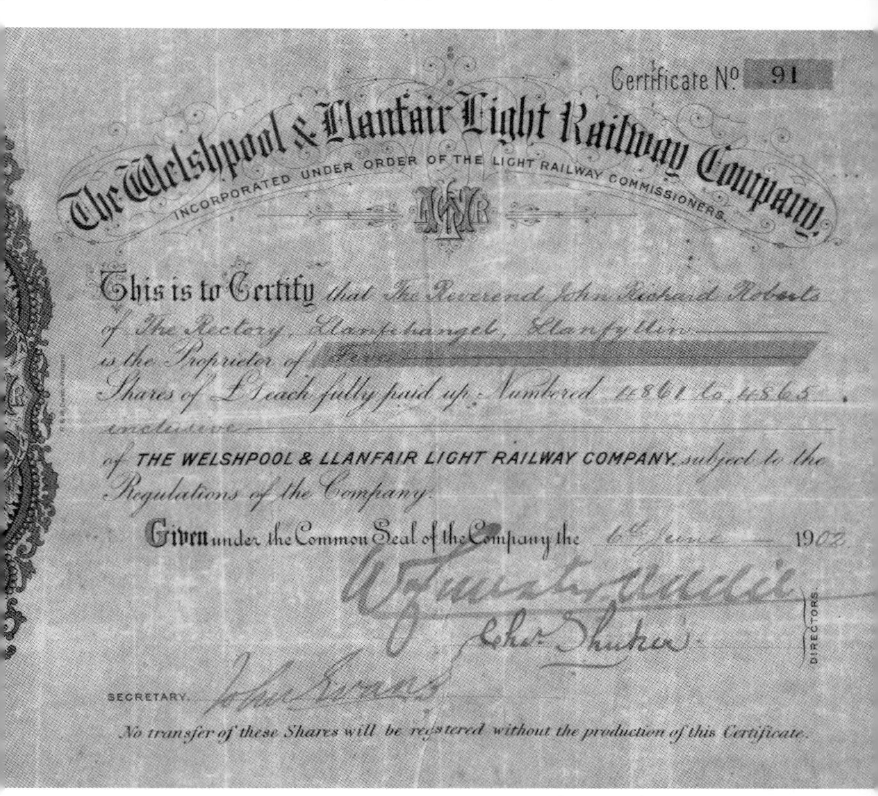
Certificate No. 91

The Welshpool & Llanfair Light Railway Company.

INCORPORATED UNDER ORDER OF THE LIGHT RAILWAY COMMISSIONERS.

This is to Certify that The Reverend John Richard Roberts of The Rectory, Llanfihangel, Llanfyllin is the Proprietor of Five Shares of £1 each fully paid up Numbered 4861 to 4865 inclusive of THE WELSHPOOL & LLANFAIR LIGHT RAILWAY COMPANY, subject to the Regulations of the Company.

Given under the Common Seal of the Company the 6th June 1902.

DIRECTORS.

Chas. Shuker

SECRETARY. John Evans

No transfer of these Shares will be registered without the production of this Certificate.

Share Certificate No. 91 for the Welshpool and Llanfair Light Railway Company, dated 6 June 1902. On 3 April 1903 the Board of Trade declared itself satisfied with the line and issued certificate No. R3680 for the Welshpool to Llanfair Caereinion Light Railway. The following day the line was opened. Although the line was well used at first, the company suffered financial difficulties from the outset. In 1909 the first cuts in the service were introduced. After the Railways Act of 1921 the line was taken over by the Great Western Railway Company. Owing to the expensive running costs they decided to close the line to passenger transport in 1931. In 1956 British Rail decided to close the line altogether.

The opening of the Welshpool and Llanfair Light Railway on 4 April 1903. From the early 1950s there had been an idea to acquire the railway for preservation. A preservation society and later a company were founded and on 6 April 1963 the Welshpool to Llanfair Light Railway was reopened by the Earl of Powis. In Welshpool, however, the line had to terminate at Raven Square and the final rails of the line through the town were lifted in 1965. Despite financial problems in the beginning the Welshpool to Llanfair Light Railway is now run under a paid general manager, and a huge group of enthusiastic volunteers provides enjoyment for thousands of visitors every year.

A Llanfair train crossing Church Street, when the line was still in use on a commercial basis.

Severn Stars station at Brook Street and Union Street, showing the Forden RDC Foden steam engine.

'On the Llanfair Railway.' Everyday life goes on in Brook Street while the light railway engine and carriages drive through Welshpool on their way to Llanfair Caereinion.

Seven Stars station in 1922. This station had no platform, but there was an open lean-to shed with a bench.

*Six*

# Education

A class of boys. National schools for boys and girls were established in Welshpool in 1821. The schools were situated on the canal side of Berriew Road. Some of the buildings are now demolished but one red brick building remains.

A class of girls from the National School.

*Above*: Christ Church choir outside the church.

*Right*: Welshpool Grammar School was situated opposite the National Schools in Berriew Street. After the Second World War it became the Boys' Club and today is the Masonic Hall.

Welshpool Grammar School.

A class from Welshpool Grammar School, c. 1900.

Another class from Welshpool Grammar School.

A class from Christ Church School, *c.* 1912. This was situated next to Christ church, and today is a private residence.

A class from a private school in Berriew Road. The building is now a private residence.

A football team from the private school in Berriew Road, c. 1915.

A woodwork class from the National School, 1916. The woodwork classes were held in the old Grammar School opposite.

The County Intermediate School was opened in June 1898. In the 1950s it became Welshpool Grammar School and later Maesydre Primary School.

CKR was here 1941 - 44

The County Intermediate School.

A class from the County Intermediate School.

*Seven*

# Organizations and Clubs

Women members of St John's Ambulance Brigade between 1900 and 1910.

Women members of St John's Ambulance Brigade in the early twentieth century.

Women and girl members of St John's Ambulance Brigade, c. 1952.

Girl members of St John's Ambulance Brigade, c. 1961.

Red Cross cadets in the early twentieth century.

Red Cross cadets, *c.* 1911.

Red Cross ladies in the early twentieth century.

Red Cross ladies.

Red Cross personnel and St John's Ambulance Brigade members, c. 1940.

An ambulance belonging to the Red Cross and St John's Ambulance Brigade serving with the British Army in the Middle East during the First World War.

Women's football team from the day shift of the Munitions Factory housed in the old flannel mill by the Montgomery Canal. This photograph dates from the First World War.

A group of employees from the Munitions Factory during the First World War.

Members of Welshpool Horticultural Society, 1905.

yvonne Jones + Connie Bowen

The YMCA mobile library with members of Welshpool Town Council in the 1940s.

Members of the Ancient Order of Foresters outside the Town Hall in 1952.

Welshpool Field Club on an outing on Llanymynech Hill. The Field Club arranged trips in the countryside and collected information about local flora and fauna.

Welshpool Field Club outside Pant Chapel House.

The Field Club in 1909.

Another outing with the Field Club.

A match on Victoria Bowling Green, *c.* 1930.

The Victoria Bowling Green.

A group of Welshpool citizens at the beginning of the twentieth century.

*Eight*

# Special Events

Powys Eisteddfod held at Castle Domen in Welshpool in 1906. The first record of a gathering similar to an eisteddfod is from 1176, when the Lord Rhys of Deheubarth (South Wales) held a large Christmas party at which poets and musicians were invited to compete. Like today the competition was proclaimed twelve months in advance and prizes were awarded.

Powys Eisteddfod, 1906. The tradition of the eisteddfod continued during the Middle Ages, but from the end of the sixteenth century Welsh poetry declined, and although eisteddfods still took place the venues were pubs and taverns rather than manor houses and courts.

Eisteddfod group in the 1930s in front of Christ church. During the eighteenth century the eisteddfod tradition almost disappeared, but a young man named Tom Jones, with the support of the Gwyneddigion Society, breathed new life into the eisteddfod and the tradition was restored by the last decade of the eighteenth century. It was at the 1858 Llangollen Eisteddfod that the idea was developed to organize a national eisteddfod. At a public meeting during the Denbigh Eisteddfod in 1860 the rules and regulations of the new organization were laid down and a council of twenty members was elected. In August 1861 the first Royal National Eisteddfod was held in Aberdare. There were several administrative and financial problems during the first twenty years of the organization's existence, but in 1880 a National Eisteddfod Association was formed and since then, except in 1914, a Royal National Eisteddfod has been held every year, alternating between North and South Wales.

The Perambulation of the Boundaries of the Borough of Welshpool took place from 4 to 7 September 1906. This shows the third day at Trewern. Very little is known of this tradition. In a document dating from before 1907 it is stated that the Perambulation 'commences on Leighton Bridge–this occupying the ford where the turnpike road crosses from Pool to Leighton, as mentioned in the description of the boundary made in 1818 ...'. Very detailed instructions follow, including walking along the River Severn, following specific hedges and streams, changing direction by trees particularly marked, and finishing 'along the south eastern sides of Little and Big Moors to where they join the turnpike road leading from Welshpool to Shrewsbury'.

A halt during the Perambulation proceedings of 1906. This walk seems to have been an excuse for picnics, games and generally having a good time.

At Cwm Dingle for the Perambulation.

By the river during the 1906 Perambulation.

Tug of war at the Perambulation.

*Right*: Memorial for those who fell in the First World War. This was unveiled by the Archbishop of Wales on 24 April 1923 and it stands outside St Mary's church.

*Below:* Declaration of the poll on 31 May 1929, showing people in Broad Street heading towards the Town Hall. Montgomeryshire has always been a Liberal constituency, except for the years 1979 to 1983 when a Conservative MP represented the county.

Declaration of the poll on the balcony of the Town Hall, 31 May 1929. From left to right: Clement Davies KC (Liberal MP), Mrs Davies (his wife), C. Thomas (the Liberal agent), the High Sheriff, the Hon. Mrs Naylor, J.N. Naylor (Conservative candidate), Mrs Evans, John Evans (Labour candidate).

Welshpool Bazaar in the Town Hall, 27 October 1938.

Ladies dressed up, early 1950s.

*Left*: A poster advertising a horse show in Welshpool on 14 September 1899.

*Below*: Horse sale at the paddock, part of the Smithfield Market, which is now a car park.

BOOK THE DATE

# HORSE RACING

AT

# WELSHPOOL

(On the border of England and Wales)

Main G.W. Line from Birmingham, Liverpool
and Manchester to Aberystwyth

# EASTER MONDAY

MARCH 29th, 1948

## OVER £400 IN PRIZES

SIX OPEN RACES, INCLUDING

# £125 OPEN RACE

FURTHER PARTICULARS LATER

County Times, Printers, Welshpool

Horse racing at Welshpool on 29 March 1948. On 21 September 1645 the first race meeting was held at Cofnybran near Llanfyllin to commemorate the visit of Charles I to Llanfyllin. The races were stopped during the years of Oliver Cromwell because his Puritan government disapproved of gambling, but with the restoration of the monarchy the races were run again in 1660, continuing until 1803 when they were transferred to Oswestry. Racing also took place in Newtown and Montgomery.

Horses on sale at the paddock.

Thanksgiving service for the restoration of St Mary's church in 1963, led by the bishop of St Asaph.

*Nine*

# Royal Visits

*Above*: Prince Edward (later Edward VII) and his wife Alexandra stopped at Welshpool on 25 June 1896. They were on their way to Aberystwyth where the prince was to be installed as the first Chancellor of the University of Wales. The royal party was met at Welshpool station by the mayor, the directors and chief officials of the Cambrian Railways, the Montgomeryshire Militia, a special choir of two hundred voices and other invited guests. In the background is the banner welcoming the royal couple: 'Our lost Llewelyn seems again to come/For love of learning to his ancient home.'

*Left*: Queen Victoria's Diamond Jubilee. An unknown lady is standing by her bicycle, decorated to celebrate the occasion.

Queen Victoria's Diamond Jubilee. The procession in Welshpool took place in June 1897. In this photograph, one of three taken minutes apart, the parade has just reached the Town Hall at 10.28 a.m. It is led by the band of the Montgomeryshire Militia 4th Battalion South Wales Borderers and followed by the permanent staff of the Militia, the Welshpool Squadron of the Montgomeryshire Yeomanry and the Welshpool 'C' Company of the 5th Volunteer Battalion, South Wales Borderers.

More from the Jubilee. This photograph was taken at approximately 10.30 a.m. The military regiments have passed and the procession is now of children. Notice how black umbrellas are used to shade the delicate white skins of many of the ladies.

Celebrating Queen Victoria. At approximately 10.36 a.m. the parade has almost finished passing the Town Hall. The last people are the Corporation officials and members of the Welshpool Lodge of Freemasons No. 998.

Visit by the Prince and Princess of Wales, 1909. This gateway was erected on the Canal Bridge in Severn Street.

Shooting party at Lymore. On 25 November 1909 the Prince and Princess of Wales (later King George V and Queen Mary) were the guests of the Earl of Powis at Lymore Hall. This was originally a hunting lodge but was rebuilt in 1675 by Edward, 3rd Lord Herbert of Chirbury. Later it was used by the Lords of Powis.

Gathering of a procession outside the railway station to celebrate the coronation of King George V and Queen Mary on June 1911. The crowd includes members of the Montgomeryshire Yeomanry and several school classes.

Berriew Coronation Ringers. For the coronation of George V these fine gentlemen were chosen to ring the bells of Berriew parish church.

Visit by the Prince of Wales, later Edward VIII, to Welshpool in July 1923.

*Ten*

# The Montgomeryshire Yeomanry Cavalry

Montgomeryshire Yeomanry parade passing through Severn Street at the turn of the century. By the beginning of the nineteenth century Britain was threatened both from abroad and internally. Napoleon was building up an army and a navy on the other side of the channel, which was thought to indicate a possible French invasion of Britain. At the same time low wages, bad harvests and thereby rising prices, heavy military expenses resulting in more taxes and a financial recession gave ample reasons for social unrest in most of the country. In 1801 the Goverment decided to call out all military forces and encouraged volunteers to form troops. In 1801 the male population of Montgomeryshire was 23,000; of these the regular militia force consisted of 475 men, the local militia force of 350 men and there were 1,680 volunteers. From these volunteers 120 men formed three troops of cavalry, to be named the Montgomeryshire Yeomanry Cavalry in 1803.

Montgomeryshire Yeomanry at Tyn-Y-Coed in 1906. The first three troops were the Montgomery troop led by Captain Arthur Davies Owen, the Welshpool troop commanded by Captain John Williams and the Newtown/Abermule troop commanded by Captain the Revd John Pryce. A new Berriew troop was added in 1813, and in 1819 two new troops joined from Llangedwyn and Llanfyllin.

Montgomeryshire Yeomanry parade. In 1803 the Lieutenant-Colonel was Charles Watkin Williams Wynn, who supported the troops financially. The uniform was scarlet with black facings and remained so for the next 120 years, although the design changed several times. The arms were swords and pistols. The badge was the red dragon and the motto was 'Anorchfygol' (Invincible). The headquarters were in Welshpool and the parade ground was Trehelig Ground.

At Tyn–Y–Coed in 1906. After the Battle of Trafalgar and Nelson's victory, the threat of a French invasion was removed and the infantry troops created out of the 1,680 volunteers were transferred to the local militia. This left the Yeomanry as a totally separate body.

A field kitchen of the Montgomeryshire Yeomanry Cavalry. The training of the cavalry troops took place on a rather irregular basis, but the Yeomanry were called out in 1819 when political and social unrest threatened the ruling classes of the county.

A rifle shooting match between the Montgomeryshire Yeomanry and the 7th Royal Welsh Fusiliers, *c.* 1910. In March 1828 the Government decided to break up the cavalry to save public funds. However, two years later further unrest and riots forced the Government to agree to the re-formation of the Montgomeryshire Yeomanry Cavalry, with a final total of four troops from Newtown, Montgomery, Welshpool and Llangedwyn.

A parade of the Montgomeryshire Yeomanry in Machynlleth, *c.* 1910. By the end of the 1830s the Chartist movement (demanding democratic reforms and social justice) had gained so much support in Montgomeryshire that it was considered a threat to the authorities, and the Montgomeryshire Yeomanry were called out to maintain law and order.

Montgomeryshire Yeomanry 'D' Squadron arriving at Hay from Llandrindod Wells in August 1914. In the autumn of 1838 the Montgomeryshire Yeomanry Cavalry were in a more peaceful mood when they escorted Princess Victoria and her mother the Duchess of Kent during their visit to the county.

Montgomeryshire Yeomanry 'D' Squadron during active service in 1914. The man on the right is a dispatch rider.

Christmas 1914, celebrated with a bottle of whisky. During the second half of the nineteenth century the Montgomeryshire Yeomanry Cavalry changed lieutenant-colonel several times. It was reorganized in 1862 when two more troops were added, again in 1889, and in 1892 a Guilsfield troop was added. In 1893 Llanfyllin and Llangedwyn formed one troop, Welshpool and Guilsfield another, and Newtown and Berriew a third.

Active service, 1914. By the end of the nineteenth century regular training took place and the cavalry met once a year for a week or more of exercises. When the Prince and Princess of Wales visited Machynlleth in June 1896, part of their escort was made up of members of the Montgomeryshire Yeomanry Cavalry.

Active service, 1914. Most of the existing photographs of the Montgomeryshire Yeomanry Cavalry date from the First World War.

Active service, 1914. On 11 October 1899 war was declared between Great Britain and the Transvaal and Orange Free State Republics. In December of the same year the Montgomeryshire Yeomanry Cavalry were called up to serve in the war.

Church parade, 1914. On 13 March 1900, after training at Wynnstay at the expense of H.L. Watkin Williams Wynn, who also equipped them, two companies – in all 232 men – boarded the SS *Montrose* in Liverpool and arrived in South Africa less than a month later. A further forty-nine men joined them later the same year. The troops were involved in much fighting and after a year had taken part in sixty actions, during which eight men died.

Active service, 1914.

Active service, 1914. At the start of the war in South Africa employers in Britain agreed to keep employment open for the fighting men for a year. In 1901 some of the men decided to stay on and some returned to be replaced by two companies from Montgomeryshire, who had left Southampton on 6 April 1901 on the SS Norman and arrived in South Africa by the end of that same month. These troops too saw heavy fighting, and nine died before the war ended in the summer of 1901.

Montgomeryshire Yeomanry 'B' Squadron: sergeants and sergeant majors in Dorchester, 1915.

'A' Squadron of the Montgomeryshire Yeomanry at Blickling Hall, near Aylsham in Norfolk, in 1915. In 1901 the cavalry was renamed the Montgomeryshire Imperial Yeomanry, only to be renamed again, in 1908, the Montgomeryshire Territorial Yeomanry. During the first decade of the twentieth century the troops still met for yearly training and were known especially for their excellent camp arrangements in picketing horses and organizing camp kitchens, as well as for their musketry.

*Left*: Montgomeryshire Yeomanry at Hayling Island in 1915. In 1914 the First World War broke out and on 4 August 1914 at 5.30 p.m. mobilization was declared. The Yeomanry consisted of four– later cut down to three– squadrons: Llanfyllin, Welshpool (broken up later), Newtown and Llandrindod Wells. They were sent for training first at Blickling Hall for a year, then to Holt Hall for about a month and finally to winter quarters in Cromer.

*Below*: Boxing match in 'C' Squadron, 1915.

Watering horses: the Montgomeryshire Yeomanry during the First World War. On 3 September the Yeomanry were sent to Egypt where they fought the Turks in several heavy battles and advanced into Palestine. During the stay in Egypt they were amalgamated with the Welsh Horse Regiment to form the 25th Battalion Royal Welch Fusiliers, which meant that they lost their commanding officer, Colonel R.W. Williams Wynn. On 30 April 1918 the troops left Egypt for Marseilles and for the rest of the war they took part in the defeat of the German army. They were at the Somme, the Hindenburg line and at Epehy among other battles, and they were fighting when the armistice was declared, on 11 November 1918, at 11 a.m.

Boxing match in Norfolk during the First World War. During the war reserve troops had been built up in Montgomeryshire, and some of the men had been sent to the front. The Montgomeryshire Yeomanry lost twenty-four officers and ninety-two men. Owing to financial problems and the decreasing importance of the horse in warfare the Yeomanry were disbanded in 1919. The cavalry held their last parade on 20 September 1920 in Welshpool.

*Eleven*

# The Surrounding Area

Powis Castle from private walks. The castle was built by the princes of Upper Powys during the Middle Ages. Since 1587 it has belonged to the Herbert family, and later the Clive family—including Lord Clive of India.

The gardens of Powis Castle are said to have been laid out by William Winde. The gardens incorporate Italian and French styles and include statues, an orangery, an aviary, and many rare plants and flowers.

Powis Castle, the inner courtyard. The earls of Powis have always dominated the area, being involved in the governing of the town, the building of the canal and the railways, and running several businesses.

Powis Castle from the gardens. During the Civil War the then Lord Powis sided with Charles I. However, the castle was besieged and surrendered to the parliamentary forces, led by Sir Thomas Myddelton.

*Above*: The tapestry drawing-room of Powis Castle. The castle is now run by the National Trust, which has set up the Clive Museum, which shows the treasures brought back from India by Lord Clive of India and his son.

*Left*: Fireplace and mantelpiece at Powis Castle. The interior of the castle dates back to the alterations made by Sir Edward Herbert during the reign of Elizabeth I and incorporates changes made by later generations.

In the gardens of Powis Castle. There are four terraces in the gardens, each 200 yards long and decorated with statues and a wealth of flowers and plants.

The 4th Earl of Powis, George Charles Herbert, is photographed by the King or Champion Oak in Powis Castle Park after it had fallen in 1939. The oak was said to be approximately nine hundred years old. In August 1939 it had been measured by the English Arboricultural Society. It was found to be 105 feet high with a ground girth of 31 feet 7 inches and a total cubic content of 2,026 cubic feet.

On the Forden Road outside Welshpool, during one of many floods.

Sarn-Y-Bryncaled cottages on the Welshpool to Newtown Road. These were built in the early to mid-nineteenth century. Opposite them a relief road has been built, and during this work a Bronze Age ritual site was excavated. The site was interpreted as a timber circle in the tradition of Stonehenge. In the centre was buried a large pottery urn with the remains of cremated bones and four flint arrowheads.

The village of Berriew lies five to six miles from Welshpool. It has several half-timbered buildings dating back to the Middle Ages and has in recent times been the winner of the 'most beautiful village in Wales' competition.

*Above:* Llanerchydol Lodge, near Raven Square. The lodge belonged to Llanerchydol Hall, which was built in 1776.

*Left:* The Abbot's Mill, an old windmill at Trelydan. It is mentioned in the borough charter of 1406 and was probably built by the Cistercian monks of the Strata Marcella Abbey. The last miller left in 1816. The mill was destroyed by explosives in 1914 by the owner, Mr William Gitting, to make way for a road.

The village of Guilsfield is around three miles from Welshpool. It has grown dramatically during the last twenty years with a considerable number of new housing estates.

The Oak public house in Guilsfield is one of two pubs in the village, the other one being The King's Head.

Dommin's Mill (Melin-y-Domen). This was the mill of the Earl of Powis. It was built close to the motte-and-bailey castle of Domen, from which it takes its name. The mill was destroyed to make way for the railway.

Gungrog Farm, now lying on the outskirts of a housing estate.

Buttington church, situated on the road from Welshpool to Shrewsbury. This is a medieval building restored in the eighteenth century.

*Left*: Leighton church, built by John Naylor as part of his estate.

*Below*: Leighton Hall lies outside Welshpool. It was built in 1851 by John Naylor, a wealthy Liverpool banker. The interior was designed by William Pugin, and owing to its resemblance to the Houses of Parliament is often used by television and film companies. The hall was part of a large estate including a parish church and farm which were lit by gas from the estate's own gasworks.

John Naylor was a pioneer in agriculture. His farm made use of all the newest innovations, including waterworks driving turbines to power machinery. On a hill he had built a liquid fertilizer tank, which distributed its contents to the fields through a system of pipes. The tank was filled by a funicular railway.

# Acknowledgements

All of the photographs in this book are from the collection of the Powysland Museum and Montgomeryshire Canal Centre in Welshpool, and thanks therefore should go to all donors who have given photographs to the museum. Thanks are also due to the Town Council of Welshpool, which holds the copyright to some of the photographs.

I would like to thank the following for their generous help: Sheila Andrew, Dr Chris Arnold, Terence Challinor, the staff of Clwyd-Powys Archaeological Trust, Christine Jones, Mrs Rachel Palmer and the staff at Welshpool Library.